Passing
Thoughts
Of Christmas

Passing Thoughts of Christmas

D. G. Hull

TATE PUBLISHING
AND ENTERPRISES, LLC

Published by Tate Publishing & Enterprises, LLC
127 E. Trade Center Terrace | Mustang, Oklahoma 73064 USA
1.888.361.9473 | www.tatepublishing.com

Tate Publishing is committed to excellence in the publishing industry. The company reflects the philosophy established by the founders, based on Psalm 68:11,
"The Lord gave the word and great was the company of those who published it."

Book design copyright © 2014 by Tate Publishing, LLC. All rights reserved.

Published in the United States of America

ISBN: 978-1-63268-146-1
1. Drama/Religious & Liturgical
2. Poetry/ Subjects & Themes/Inspirational & Religious
14.03.07

This collection of poems represents
random thoughts of Christmas
that have passed through the mind
of the author, from time to time.
Thoughts that tend to look at the
Christmas story in unconventional ways.
He hopes you will enjoy them and that
they may give you pause for thought.

A Humble Stall

In a manger in a humble stall...
Our Saviour came to save us all.
The shepherds watching had no clue...
To what this little child would do.

They couldn't know or be aware...
Of the heavy burdens He would bear.
To suffer anguish, pain and loss...
To take our place upon the cross.

They simply did as they were told...
By angels speaking clear and bold.
To go and worship child and King...
The one who'd take away sin's sting.

As humble shepherds, too, are we...
Sometimes it's hard for us to see...
That God's most gracious gift of all...
Was in a manger in a humble stall

In the Middle of a Night Sky

(a Christmas reading)

In the middle of a night sky
In a land far away
A star watched a weary couple
Who had no place to stay.

In the middle of a night sky
In a land far away
A star shone on a stable
Where a little baby lay.

In the middle of a night sky
In a land far away
A star was joined by angels
With joyous things to say.

In the middle of a night sky
In a land far away
A star watched humble shepherds
Seek a King who slept on hay.

In the middle of a night sky
In a land far away
A star led curious travellers
So they wouldn't go astray.

In the middle of a night sky
In a land far away
A star announced a Savior
Who would take our sins away.

In the middle of a night sky
In a land far away
A star could not shine bright enough
To match the love of God that day.

Standing Tall

The Christmas tree stands tall and bright...
In the church's humble hall.
It sheds a warm and calming light
On each and every wall.

The children have all gone by now...
Their songs have all been sung.
The worshipers have all gone home...
There are stocking to be hung.

The church is locked and left alone...
The tree lights were left on.
The twinkling of those tiny lights...
Will greet the Christmas dawn.

The sunlight of the brand new day...
Seems to dim the Christmas tree.
But, even though the lights grow dim...
There's a lesson for you and me.

Whether all alone or in a crowd...
In a dark corner or on display...
The Good News of our Saviour's birth...
Should be shared by us each day

The following is a Christmas program
including children elementary
through middle school age.
Use your imagination as to staging, etc.
The songs are only suggestions...
use whatever music you prefer.

"You're Just a Star....That's All You Are!"

main characters: Sheep Twins(Shannon & Sherman...*want to believe*)
Old Sheep (*wise...knows the 'story'*)
Other Sheep(8-10)(ex: #1-#2-#3-etc. or names...
Ralphie...Felice...Wilber... Marjorie...*they aredoubtful*)
Shepherds (2)(*perplexed*)
Angel Choir (6-12?)(*sings from time to time*)
Little Lambs (pre-schoolers...*cute & funny*)
Scene One:
(a flock of sheep on a hillside, outside of Bethlehem)
(it's late at night...all but two sheep are asleep...)
(lights come up on main characters...the Twins...
(they are gazing up at the sky...)

Sherman: You're just a star... **Shannon:** ...that's all you are...
Sherman: Nothing special...nothing great...
Shannon: No cause for us to stay up late...
Sherman: We don't believe the Old Sheep's story...
Shannon: 'Bout God's son and heaven's glory...
Sherman: It seems far fetched...**Shannon:** It's just a tale...
Sherman: Told by an Old Sheep...**Shannon:** With a crooked tail.

9

Sheep 1: Oh great...oh thanks you've woke us up again.

Sheep 2: Just for giggles...let's pretend...

Sheep 3: That when it's dark we go to sleep...

Sheep 3: And if you need some help...just...uh...count...um...sheep?

Sherman: Fine...OK...we'll just lie down...

Shannon: We'll just ignore your tired frowns

Sherman: But, we don't expect to fall asleep...

Shannon: Even if we count all us sheep!

      (they both look back up at the sky)

Sherman & Shannon: You're just a star...that's all you are...YAWN...~(they fall asleep and dream of angels)~ ~(Angel Choir recites scripture ... "For unto us..."..then sings...? "It Came Upon a Midnight Clear"?)~

           ~(Angels exit)~

   ~(two shepherds come by to investigate 'voices')~

Shepherd 1: Did you hear talking?

Shepherd 2: No...not me.

Shepherd 2: I think there's nothing here to see.

Shepherd 1: But, I am sure that I heard voices!

Shepherd 2: Well...these hills are full of noises.

Scene Two: (it's morning!)

Sheep ?: Well...look at you two you've opened your eyes...

Sheep ?: You spent too much time looking up at the skies...

Sheep ?: The rest of us sheep have been up for hours...

Sheep ?: If you sleep too long you'll get covered with flowers!

Old Sheep: I think it just might be, young friends...

A dreamy night is at an end...

These wooly twins have much to tell...

It's nothing new...I know it well.

Sheep ?: Tell us dreamers of your dream..

Sheep ?: Just how real does it really seem?

Sheep ?: Did you dream about the star?

Old Sheep: And those who seek it from afar?

Sherman: Yes we did......

Shannon: ...how did you know?...

Sherman: We did dream of the bright star's glow....

Shannon: There were three who sought the star...

Sherman: And yes they travelled very far.

(someone sings...'We Three Kings')

Old Sheep: The story's been told from sheep to lamb...

About the God known as *I am*...

How someday He would send His Son...

To be born in a stable...plain as anyone.

Sheep ?: All this talk is so confusing...

Sheep ?: At times it almost seems amusing...

Sheep ?: How are we to understand...

Sheep ?: Something quite so great and grand?

Sheep ?: Here come the little lambs at play...

Sheep ?: Let's ask them what they have to say...

Sheep ?: Tell us lambies what you saw...

Little Lambs: Baa...baa...baa...baa...baa...baa...baa!

~(sheep look at each other as if to say...'what?')

~(Little Lambs sing...)~

11

Scene Three:
(lights slowly dim...it's evening)
Sherman: Well that was nice...
Shannon: ...they're all so sweet...
Sherman: To hear them sing was quite a treat...
Shannon: But now our day is done it seems...
Old Sheep: Time for sleep and dreaming dreams.
Sheep ?: Oh. look you two...your star is out...
Sheep ?: I still don't see what the fuss is about!
Sherman: It seems much brighter...
Shannon: ...and closer, too...
Sherman: Could there be something...
Shannon: ...that we should do?
Old Sheep: I think that we should watch and wait...
              Tonight's a night to stay up late...
              This could be the special night...
              To see God's glory...shinning bright!
                    ~(song)~
Sherman: Look at the star it's shinning down...
Shannon: Down upon little Bethlehem town.
Sheep ?: You two weren't crazy...
Sheep ?: now it seems...
Sheep ?: Strange things are happening..
Sheep ?: like in your dreams!
     ~(someone sings...'O Littlte Town of Bethlehem')~
Sherman: I'm sort of scared...
Shannon: But soooo excited...
Old Sheep: Look there..the three the star has guided...

12

Sherman & Shannon: It's like our dream is coming true...Old Sheep...Old Sheep...what should we do?
(All the sheep are getting very excited)
Sheep ?: The sky is full of the brightest light...
Sheep ?: Even though it's late at night.
Sheep ?: Look there's a gazillion angels singing...
Sheep ?: Listen to the GOOD NEWS their bringing!
       ~ (song...'Hark the Herald?)~
       ~(Shepherds rush in...also excited)~
Shepherd 1: Come on you sheep...
Shepherd 2: ...come with us!!
Shepherd 1: We're going to town...
Shepherd 2: ...to see what's the buzz!!
Shepherd 1: With all these angels in the sky...
Shepherd 2: ...we don't know what to think...Oh My!!
       ~(Shepherds and sheep exit quickly...
       except for Sherman, Shannon and Old Sheep)~
     ~ (Old Sheep is somewhat upstage(back)watching the
       twins with a smile) (Sherman & Shannon are front
and
       center...they look up at the star)~
Sherman: It seems too much for us to take...
Shannon: Pinch me and see if I'm awake...
Sherman: To think our dreams were of God's plan...
Shannon: Of peace on earth...good will to man.
       ~(short pause)(They look up)~
Sherman & Shannon: You're the most special star...that's what you are!!
    ~(All three exit, as did the others) (Lights go down)~
       ~THE END~

A LITTLE BITTY BABY

A little bitty baby was
　　　　born in a manger
A little bitty baby was
　　　　pretty much a stranger
Nobody knew him...
　　　　except his Mom and Dad
Nobody knew
　　　　the potential that he had.

Before he was born
　　　　his folks traveled far
It wasn't very easy
　　　　'cause they didn't have a car
His Mom rode a donkey...
　　　　his Dad had to walk
They didn't have a radio
　　　　so all they did was talk.

When they arrived in Bethlehem...
　　　　people filled the town
They couldn't find a place to stay...
　　　　up street or down
At the point of giving up
　　　　they stopped at one more place
The keeper of the inn said...
　　　　he just might have some space.

The space he had was not so nice...
they didn't really mind
Because the baby's time had come
they took what they could find.

There inside that stable stall
his Mom made him a bed
He slept all wrapped in swaddling clothes
with straw around his head
While he slept some shepherds came
and knelt there in the straw
They told the baby's parents
of all the sights they saw.

The shepherds told a story
that was hard to believe
They said a bunch of angels t
old them they should leave
Go into the town, they said,
and seek a baby boy
When you look into his eyes
he'll fill your hearts with joy.

The angels pointed to the star
that shone above the town
They said you'll find the baby boy
where the beams come down
So off they went and sure enough
there within the glow
They found the little bitty boy
wrapped from head to toe.

16

Some time later, so it's told,
     three men so rich and wise
Stopped to see the little boy
     and couldn't believe their eyes
They had traveled many miles
     for days and months and years
To find the savior God had sent...
     this brought them all to tears.

We like them should be in awe
     and praise the Lord above
Because that little bitty baby came
     to demonstrate God' love
So...whether you're a shepherd
     or your very wise and rich
God sent His son to save your soul...
     it doesn't matter which.

Think about this story...
     think about that boy
Think about how much He wants
     to share eternal joy
That little bitty baby
     was born in a manger
That little bitty baby...
     don't let Him be a stranger.

(Some Xmas wRap)

People...people listen up.......
I need your attention...
I got some stuff *(thoughts)* up in my head.......
I really need to mention.

2000 years ago or so.......
a saviour child was born.......
He came to take our sins away.......
and all the world forewarn.......

That someday He'd come back this way.......
In glory He'd be seen
To take believers up with Him.......
to heaven's what I mean.

Yeah, like a shepherd with his flock.......
He'll sort 'em out someday.......
The sheep will all be safe and sound.......
the goats He'll say "No way!!"

But, now I've gone and jumped ahead.......
to what will be someday.......
*(Right)*Now's the time we need to think*(hear)*.......
about that baby on the hay.

I won't take too much precious time.......
I'm sure you've heard the tale.......
The star, the shepherds, the wisemen, three.......
(An) Expectant couple on the trail.

You've heard it nearly all your life.......
every year about this time.......
You read it in the Holy Book.......
you hear it set in rhyme.

So, when you shop for Christmas gifts.......
and trim your Christmas tree.......
Don't forget the Christmas story.......
and what God gave you and me!